This book belongs to:

_____

_____

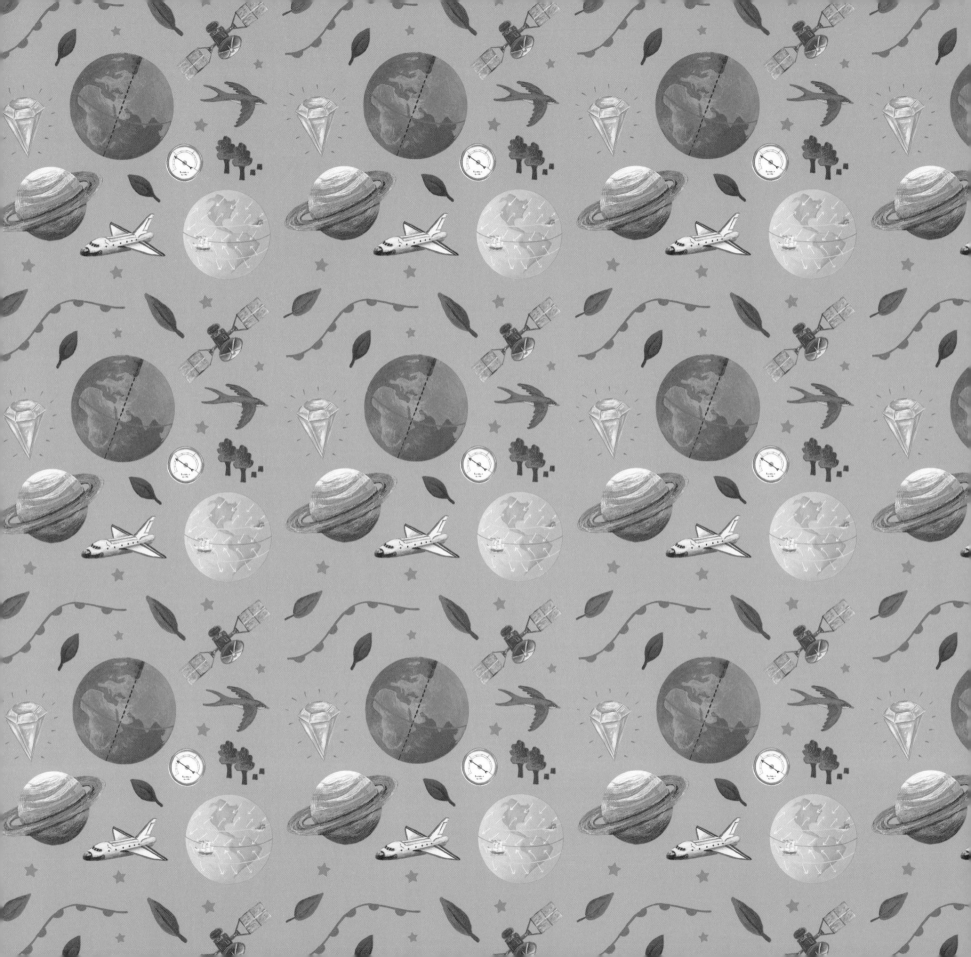

To Phil, Tom, and Nico —CD

First US edition in this format 2024
First published in this format by Templar Books, an imprint of Bonnier Books UK, 2023

Library of Congress Catalog Card Number 2009031057
ISBN 978-1-5362-3575-3

24 25 26 27 28 29 TLF 10 9 8 7 6 5 4 3 2 1

Printed in Dongguan, Guangdong, China

This book was typeset in Albus, Aristelle Sans, Billy, Bokka Solid, Cute Be Special, and Kidprint MT Pro.
The illustrations were done in acrylic.

TEMPLAR BOOKS
an imprint of
Candlewick Press
99 Dover Street
Somerville, Massachusetts 02144

www.candlewick.com

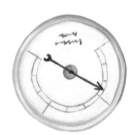

HOW THE WORLD WORKS

Christiane Dorion • *illustrated by* **Beverley Young**

templar books
an imprint of Candlewick Press

What on earth happened?

We live on a unique planet, which travels around one of billions of stars in our universe. But how did it all begin? Astronomers think that 13.7 billion years ago, the whole universe emerged from a tiny invisible dot. Mind-boggling, isn't it?

The sun

The sun is the closest star to us and is at the center of our solar system. It is a massive ball of burning gas that produces light and heat. Without the sun, there would be no life on Earth.

The planets

Eight planets travel around, or orbit, the sun at different speeds, rotating like spinning tops. The four planets closest to the sun, including Earth, are made of rocks and metals. The four outer planets are bigger and are made of gas.

So, which planet is which?
1. Mercury 2. Venus
3. Earth 4. Mars
5. Jupiter 6. Saturn
7. Uranus
8. Neptune

Asteroids

Asteroids are chunks of rock left over from the formation of the solar system. Millions travel around the sun between Mars and Jupiter.

Comets

Comets are giant lumps of ice and dust that orbit the sun. As they come close to the sun, they begin to melt, leaving an impressive trail behind them.

Did you know that Pluto isn't considered a planet anymore? It's too small! It's now called a dwarf planet.

The Big Bang!

Where did all this come from?

Try to imagine the earth, the moon, the sun, the planets, and the stars all squeezed together into something so small it's invisible. This is how we think the universe started.

In less than a second, this invisible dot expanded incredibly fast, throwing out lots of dust, gas, and other particles. Over billions of years, these particles gradually stuck together to form all the stars, planets, and moons in the universe.

What goes around . . .

comes around. Over time, we have put thousands of objects into orbit around the earth to learn more about our planet and what lies beyond it.

Space station

The International Space Station is the size of a soccer field. It was built by 17 countries working together so that astronauts can live in space for months on end.

Hubble telescope

This telescope is the size of a bus. It takes photographs and collects information about the universe.

Satellites

Satellites take pictures of Earth to forecast the weather and make maps. They also bounce signals across the globe for communication, radio, and television.

Space junk

Old satellites and thousands of nuts, bolts, tools, and other objects have been left by astronauts and now orbit the earth. There's a lot of junk out there!

Why is Earth unique?

Isn't it amazing that Earth is the only planet in the solar system where we know life exists? The conditions are perfect: it's not too hot and not too cold; there is air to breathe and water to drink.

The seasons

The earth leans to one side while spinning around the sun. This tilt creates the seasons, because as the earth travels around the sun, different areas receive different amounts of sunlight.

Earth facts!

Age: Nearly 4.6 billion years

Length of year (the time it takes to orbit the sun): 365 days—or, to be precise, 365 days, 6 hours, 9 minutes, and 9.54 seconds!

Diameter: 7,926 miles/12,742 kilometers (As planets go, Earth is quite small!)

Spring

Autumn

March

It is spring in the Northern Hemisphere and autumn in the Southern Hemisphere.

June

The Northern Hemisphere leans toward the sun. It is summer in the north and winter in the south.

Summer

Winter

September

It is autumn in the Northern Hemisphere and spring in the Southern Hemisphere.

Day and night

The earth rotates once in 24 hours. As it spins, one side is lit by the sun, and it is daytime. The other side is dark, and it is nighttime. Imagine that the flashlight is the sun and the ball is the earth.

Why not try this at home with a flashlight?

Winter

Summer

December

The Northern Hemisphere points away from the sun. It is winter in the north and summer in the south.

Autumn

Spring

The moon

Our nearest neighbor in space is the moon: a huge ball of rock. The moon orbits the earth, so every night we see a different part of it lit up by the sun. This is why it seems to change shape in the sky.

What if there were no moon?

Earth would spin faster, so the days would be much shorter. The moon's gravity slows down the earth's rotation.

Gravity

If you drop something, it falls to the ground. This is because of gravity, a force that makes the objects in the universe pull toward each other. The earth's gravity pulls us toward the ground, stopping us from whizzing off into space. Gravity also keeps the planets in orbit around the sun and the moon in orbit around the earth.

When did life begin?

The answer is 3.8 billion years ago! When the earth formed (about 4.6 billion years ago), it was a lifeless ball of molten rock wrapped in poisonous gas and bombarded by meteorites. It was very dark and very hot. Millions of years later, the first signs of life appeared and changed very slowly into today's plants and animals.

Earth's history in 24 hours!

Imagine the whole history of the earth squeezed into one day. One minute would represent about 3 million years and one second, 50,000 years!

Earth forms 00:00

The molten earth slowly cools down, and its solid crust develops. Gases from volcanoes help create the atmosphere. Rain begins to fall, making oceans.

Slime! 03:57

The first forms of life appear in the ocean: tiny, slimy things called bacteria. One type of bacteria begins to produce oxygen from water.

The first bacteria appeared in the ocean 3.8 billion years ago.

Fossils help us find out about ancient plants and animals.

Animal explosion 21:40

The sea starts to fill with plants and odd-looking creatures, including sponges, coral, jellyfish, bony fish, water scorpions, and giant woodlice called trilobites.

Giant woodlice called trilobites appeared in the sea 545 million years ago.

Land plants 21:40

Plants start to grow on land. It will take millions of years for these clumps of moss to be replaced by grassy plants and leafy trees.

Plants spread over the land 440 million years ago.

Land animals 22:05

The first animals crawl out of the sea. They grow legs and learn to breathe air. Insects and reptiles appear on the scene.

The first reptiles appeared 360 million years ago. This one is called Dimetrodon.

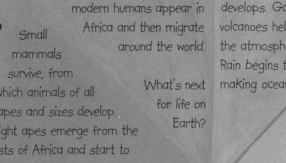

Dinosaurs 23:06

A group of huge reptiles called dinosaurs rules the world. After millions of years, a meteorite hits Earth, wiping out all the dinosaurs and many other creatures.

About 170 million years ago, the biggest reptiles of all, the dinosaurs, roamed the earth.

Mammals 23:39

Small mammals survive, from which animals of all shapes and sizes develop. Upright apes emerge from the forests of Africa and start to make tools and use fire.

The woolly mammoth and other big mammals developed 65 million years ago.

Modern humans 23:59

Less than 14 seconds before midnight, modern humans appear in Africa and then migrate around the world.

What's next for life on Earth?

How did life begin?

Nobody knows for sure. Scientists agree that a very long time ago, life sprang from chemicals floating in the oceans. What we don't know is exactly how these chemicals turned into living organisms.

Recipe for life

1. Find a planet.
It should be just the right distance from a star, so it is not too hot and not too cold. Earth is the perfect distance from the sun.

Perfect distance

2. Bring the volcanoes to a boil.
When they erupt, the surface of the planet will be covered with burning-hot lava.

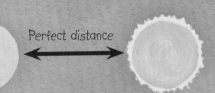

3. Add a rocky moon.
This will stop the planet from spinning too fast.

4. Add an atmosphere.
Squeeze the volcanoes to produce enough gases to create an atmosphere, which will help the planet cool down. Stir until you have the right mixture of gases, moisture, and warmth.

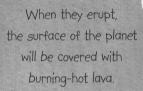

5. Cool and add water.
Cool the planet for billions of years, then throw icy comets at it. In the earth's atmosphere, the ice from the comets will turn into vapor. This will cause rain to fall, creating oceans.

Comet attack!

The oceans form.

6. Add the special ingredients for life.
Season the oceans with carbon, hydrogen, oxygen, nitrogen, a pinch of calcium, sulfur, and other elements. Mix well.

Evolution

The British scientist Charles Darwin carefully studied fossils of plants and animals. He described how living things have changed, or evolved, over millions of years to suit the different environments in which they live. In 1859, he came up with the idea that all living things, from goldfish to bananas to humans, come from one common ancestor. In a nutshell, we're all descended from slimy bacteria!

How did these chemicals turn into life?

1. Primordial soup
One idea is that life started in shallow seashore pools that contained a brew of chemicals. The theory is that lightning sparked a chemical reaction that turned simple molecules into more complex ones called amino acids—the vital ingredients for life.

2. Meteorites
Another idea is that amino acids came from meteorites hitting the planet billions of years ago.

3. Hydrothermal vents
A more recent theory is that life began near vents in the sea floor, where hot volcanic gases rich in minerals bubbled up from the earth's core. These minerals may have provided food and warmth for early forms of life.

Another theory . . .
If none of the above methods yield results, try adding an alien to the mix. Some people think that life on Earth began when aliens sent life to the planet millions of years ago.

Since humans turned up, the flightless dodo bird, the Tasmanian tiger, and many more animals have become extinct. Thousands more are about to disappear.

Pangaea

Millions of years ago, the earth's land mass looked like this.

On a map of the world, have you ever noticed that the continents could slide together like the pieces of a giant jigsaw puzzle? Scientists believe that a long time ago, the continents were joined together to form one huge land mass called Pangaea. About 200 million years ago, Pangaea began to break apart, spreading out to form today's continents.

This is how Pangaea's landscape would have looked—covered in tropical ferns and palm trees.

The continents as we know them today.

This map shows the earth's main tectonic plates. The arrows show the direction which the plates are moving.

The earth is made of different layers. The outer layer, called the crust, is broken up into big pieces called tectonic plates. These float on a thick layer of hot rock, known as the mantle, flowing inside the earth. The movement of these plates creates mountains, volcanoes, and earthquakes on the earth's surface.

Pacific Plate

North American Plate **1**

Eurasian Plate **3**

African Plate

South American Plate

2

4

Australian Plate

Antarctic Plate

IS the earth moving beneath our feet?

In a word, YES, even while you are reading this book! The earth's plates move about 1 inch each year!

How do we know that the plates move?
All over the world we can see evidence of this:

1 San Andreas Fault
The plates slide against each other, creating earthquakes.

2 Mid-Atlantic Ridge
The sea floor is spreading because the plates are moving apart, creating a long, high ridge under the sea.

3 Himalayas
These mountains were formed because two plates collided.

4 Krakatoa
This volcanic island is part of the Ring of Fire: a chain of volcanoes around the Pacific caused by plates colliding.

When plates collide . . .

When an oceanic plate moves toward a continental plate, it sinks underneath it and melts down into the mantle. The pressure forces magma up to the surface, causing volcanic eruptions. This type of collision also causes powerful earthquakes and deep ocean trenches.

	Oceanic plate
	Continental plate

This is a destructive boundary.

When two continental plates collide, the crust buckles to form mountains. As the plates continue to move toward each other, the mountains become taller.

This is a collision boundary.

When plates slide . . .

If two plates slide past each other, a huge amount of friction results, and this sudden movement creates earthquakes. More than one million quakes rattle the earth each year!

The Richter scale measures the size of an earthquake. 1 is mild; 10 is EPIC!

When plates move apart . . .

Where oceanic plates move away from each other, magma oozes up from the mantle, creating new crust between them. A chain of undersea volcanoes often forms. If a volcano rises high enough, it can form an island.

This is a conservative boundary.

This is a constructive boundary.

The world's largest active volcano is Mauna Loa in Hawaii. It has erupted over 30 times! It is taller than Mount Everest, but most of it is underwater.

Why does it rain?

The earth has a fixed amount of water that keeps going around and around in a cycle between the ocean, the air, and the ground. Water is always on the move! The sun heats the surface of rivers, lakes, and oceans, turning water into gas, or vapor. This vapor rises into the air, cools down, and turns back into water droplets (in a process called condensation). These stick to particles of dust or smoke in the air, clustering together to make clouds. Once a droplet has become heavy enough, it falls back to earth as rain or snow (precipitation). Some drops fall straight back into rivers and oceans; others run over the ground to reach them. Some drops sink slowly into the ground (infiltration), while others are soaked up by plants to evaporate again (transpiration). And then the cycle starts all over again!

Isn't it amazing that the water molecules in your body might have *been* part of a dinosaur millions of years ago?

Clouds

Condensation (water vapor becomes liquid)

Transpiration (evaporation from plants)

Evaporation (water turns into vapor)

About 10% of the vapor in the air comes from plants releasing water from their leaves.

Lake

97.5% of all the earth's water is salt water, leaving only 2.5% as fresh water!

Three-quarters of the earth's surface is covered by water.

About 2% of all the earth's water is frozen in ice caps and glaciers.

How do we get our water?

To access clean water, humans create a diversion in the water cycle. We take water from underground sources, rivers, or lakes and pump it into human-made reservoirs. This water goes to a treatment plant to be cleaned. Then it is pumped into homes, schools, offices, and factories through pipes buried in the ground. Once it has been used, dirty water goes into different underground pipes called sewers, which carry the water to the sewage plant. The water is cleaned once again and pumped back into rivers, where it continues its journey through the water cycle.

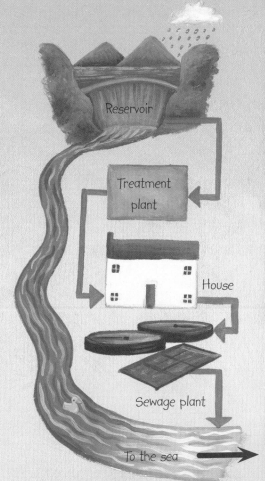

Reservoir

Treatment plant

House

Sewage plant

To the sea

Surface run-off
(water travels quickly over the ground)

A drop of water can spend 1,000 years underground!

Water table
(the upper level of groundwater)

Infiltration (Water soaks into the ground—this is very slow!)

How do we interfere with the water cycle?

Billions of plants and animals share the planet, and they all depend on water to live. But we use much more water than other species and change its quality for the worse. How do you think our actions affect the natural water cycle?

Farming

Fertilizers and pesticides can seep into rivers and lakes.

Transport

Our vehicles release harmful gases into the air. This makes the rain acidic and damages wildlife.

Spilling oil

Oil poured into drains and rivers, or leaking from cars and trucks, pollutes the water.

Logging

Chopping down forests means that rain runs quickly over the ground instead of sinking slowly into the soil.

The sun drives the weather

Less heat near the poles

The earth is round, so the sun heats some areas more than others. The air moves around to even out the temperature, creating the winds.

More heat at the equator

The earth spins in this direction.

Why does the weather change?

Simply put, the weather changes because the sun heats up different areas, driving the winds. The earth is wrapped in a layer of gas—the atmosphere. Changes in the weather happen in the lower level of the atmosphere, called the troposphere. Here, the air is always on the move, carrying heat and water around the globe.

North Pole

Easterlies

Westerlies

Horse latitudes

Trade winds

Equator

Trade winds

Horse latitudes

Westerlies

Easterlies

South Pole

The world's winds

Can you see a pattern in the way the winds blow? This pattern is created by the sun's heat and the rotation of the earth. Usually, warm air from the equator moves toward the poles, and cold air from the poles moves toward the equator. The winds do not blow in straight lines because the earth spins.

What's in a name?

The trade winds were named because ships carrying goods to trade used the winds to sail the oceans. In the horse latitudes, where winds are light, sometimes sailors were forced to throw their horses overboard when there wasn't enough wind to move a heavy ship.

Warm meets cold

Clouds and rain form when two huge air masses with different temperatures and amounts of moisture come together. The boundary between them is called a weather front.

Cold front

Warm, moist air

Cold air

Cold front

When colder air advances toward warmer air, the colder, heavier air pushes under the warmer, lighter air and forces it to rise vigorously. Cold fronts bring heavy rains followed by cool weather.

Warm front

Warm, moist air

Cold air

Warm front

When warmer air meets colder air, the warmer air rises gradually over the colder air. Warm fronts are more gentle than cold fronts, bringing light, steady rain followed by warm weather.

What's the forecast?

Thanks to information from satellites, ships, hot-air balloons, and ground instruments, meteorologists can predict the weather fairly well. But if you are planning a picnic, play it safe and take an umbrella!

Temperature

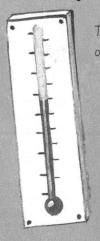

This is a measure of how hot or cold the air is. The temperature is measured in degrees Fahrenheit, Celsius, or Kelvin.

Air pressure

Air pressure is the weight of the air pressing down on the earth's surface. When warm air rises, the pressure is low. This brings clouds and rainfall. When air sinks, the pressure is high. This leads to clear skies with few clouds.

Wind speed

Wind is caused by differences in temperature and air pressure between two areas. The bigger the differences, the stronger the wind.

Predicting the weather ... naturally

Long ago, before weather forecasts existed, sailors and farmers relied on clues from nature to predict the weather. The results weren't always perfect, though!

Pinecones ...

open up when the air is dry.

Seagulls ...

fly to land when a storm is near.

Crickets ...

chirp faster in warm weather.

Cows ...

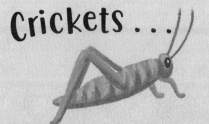

lie down on a dry patch before it rains.

What is extreme weather?

Weather can be dangerous! Winds and rain help move heat and water around the earth. But extreme weather can cause huge damage to homes, buildings, and roads and can even kill people. Scientists believe that human activities are changing our atmosphere and making the earth warmer. This might mean more extreme weather in the future!

Tornadoes

Tornadoes form when warm air gets drawn into the base of storm clouds. Like water flowing into a drain, the air rises quickly and starts spinning, sucking up everything in its path.

Hurricanes

Hurricanes are huge storms that form over warm, tropical oceans. Warm air rises and the surrounding air swirls in to take its place. As the storm gains moisture, it grows and spins faster.

Eye of the hurricane (light winds)

Extreme winds

The air above our heads can move very fast, creating gales and hurricanes. Tornadoes produce the fastest winds on Earth—sometimes traveling at close to 300 miles per hour!

Force	Description	Observation	Wind speed
0	Calm	Smoke rises up	0 mph (0 km/h)
1	Light air	Smoke drifts	1–3 mph (1–5 km/h)
2	Light breeze	Leaves rustle	4–7 mph 6–11 km/h
3	Gentle breeze	Leaves and twigs move	8–12 mph (12–19 km/h)
4	Moderate breeze	Branches move	13–18 mph (20–29 km/h)
5	Fresh breeze	Small trees sway	19–24 mph (30–39 km/h)
6	Strong breeze	Large branches move	25–31 mph (40–50 km/h)
7	Near gale	Large trees sway	32–38 mph (51–61 km/h)
8	Gale	Twigs break	39–46 mph (62–74 km/h)
9	Strong gale	Roofs damaged	47–54 mph (75–87 km/h)
10	Storm	Trees blown down	56–63 mph (88–102 km/h)
11	Violent storm	Serious damage to buildings and countryside	64–72 mph (103–117 km/h)
12	Hurricane	Violent destruction	73+ mph (118+ km/h)

The Beaufort scale is a way of measuring wind speed by looking at visible clues. It was devised in 1805 by a British naval officer named Francis Beaufort to help sailors rank wind conditions.

Why does the sea move?

Labrador current

5 2000: There are many sightings of ducks bobbing in the waves from Maine to Massachusetts.

Cold, salty water is heavier and sinks.

6 August 2003: Duck sighting in the Hebrides, Scotland.

The Gulf Stream is a powerful current that brings warm water and milder weather from the sunny tropics into the North Atlantic.

North Atlantic Gyre

Mediterranean Sea

The tides

Have you ever noticed the sea level rising and falling on the shore? This movement of water, called the tide, is caused by the moon's gravity, a force that pulls the ocean toward it. The pull of the moon makes the water rise into a high tide on one side of Earth. As the earth spins, the water also bulges on the other side. So each place on Earth has a high tide twice a day.

What if the Gulf Stream stops?

Scientists fear that global warming could affect the Gulf Stream. Melting polar ice caps will make the water at the poles less salty, preventing it from sinking and gradually slowing down the Gulf Stream. This would make Europe and North America much colder!

Atlantic Ocean

A gyre is a large, circular current at the surface of the ocean.

South Atlantic Gyre

Indian Ocean

Water flows in large, circular patterns called currents. Moving like rivers, these currents carry massive amounts of water, heat, and oxygen around the ocean. Surface currents are blown by the winds and transfer heat from warmer to cooler areas. Deep currents are created by differences in temperature and saltiness in the ocean. Colder, saltier water sinks, leaving room for warmer, less salty water to move in to replace it.

Warm, less salty water is lighter and rises.

⭐ **4** 1995-2000: Many ducks drift into the Arctic and are trapped for five years in slow-moving pack ice.

⭐ **2** November 16, 1992: First sighting of rubber ducks on the shores of Alaska.

North Pacific Gyre

⭐ **1** On January 10, 1992, a cargo ship was hit by a storm and thousands of rubber ducks were lost overboard. Scientists are following these intrepid ducks to research how currents work. Can you figure out why they landed where they did?

Garbage dump

In 1997, a scientist discovered an area of plastic rubbish twice the size of Texas, floating in a slow, swirling current in the North Pacific. It's been called the Great Pacific Garbage Patch.

Indian Ocean Gyre

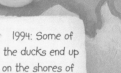

Pacific Ocean

⭐ **3** 1994: Some of the ducks end up on the shores of Australia and Indonesia.

Message in a bottle

About 310 BCE, Theophrastus, an ancient Greek philosopher, launched messages in bottles to prove that the Atlantic Ocean flowed into the Mediterranean. In the eighteenth century, the American inventor Benjamin Franklin dropped bottles in the Atlantic. The returned messages helped him create a chart of the Gulf Stream.

South Pacific Gyre

Southern Ocean

The ocean conveyor belt

Ocean currents flow in a continuous loop around the earth, like a large conveyor belt. Warm water travels from the Pacific to the Atlantic as a shallow current, and cold water flows from the Atlantic to the Pacific as a deep current.

What is carbon?

Carbon is one of the natural substances that make up everything in the world. It is in the air, the rocks, the oceans, and all living things, including you. There is a fixed amount of carbon on Earth and it is reused over and over again. Look at the natural carbon cycle below, then find out how we interfere with this cycle.

The carbon cycle

Carbon moves around all the time between the oceans, the atmosphere, the ground, and living things.

There is a constant exchange of carbon between the air and the ocean.

Carbon in the atmosphere

In the air, carbon is attached to oxygen to form a gas called carbon dioxide.

When we burn trees, carbon goes into the a...

Living things release carbon dioxide when they breathe.

Animals get their carbon from eating plants or other animals that have eaten plants.

Plants extract carbon from the air to make food.

Carbon moves from the ground to the air when rocks break down or volcanoes erupt.

Bacteria and fungi release some carbon by breaking down dead plants and animals.

When living things die, they slowly decay, putting carbon back into the soil.

Some plant and animal remains are crushed underground for millions of years, creating fossil fuels.

Did you know that diamonds are made of one of the most common substances on Earth? Carbon!

Fossil fuels

Oil, coal, and natural gas are called fossil fuels, because they come from dead plants and animals buried and crushed underground millions of years ago. We burn them to produce energy, so the gas in cars comes from living things that existed before the dinosaurs! When we burn fossil fuels, we release the carbon that was stored underground quickly into the atmosphere. This leads to climate change.

Factories and power plants release carbon from fossil fuels.

Every time we travel by car or airplane or switch on a light, we add carbon to the atmosphere.

As we cut down forests, there are fewer trees on the planet to soak up carbon from the air.

We extract oil, coal, and natural gas from the earth. We burn these fossil fuels to power factories and produce electricity.

The human influence

The world has changed quickly over the last hundred years, with an increasing number of people, factories, power plants, and cars. We are constantly adding large amounts of carbon to the air, but the planet cannot absorb it fast enough. We are meddling with the world's natural carbon cycle, with worrying results.

How is Earth like a greenhouse?

The atmosphere naturally contains gases, such as carbon dioxide, which trap heat from the sun and keep the planet warm. These are called greenhouse gases, and without them, the planet would freeze. But human activities are pumping more and more greenhouse gases into the atmosphere, so the earth is getting warmer.

The earth's atmosphere is like a greenhouse.

The natural greenhouse effect

When the sun's rays reach Earth, some are reflected back into space by the earth's surface, while greenhouse gases in the atmosphere bounce some heat back toward the earth.

Atmosphere

The human impact

Because there are more greenhouse gases in the atmosphere, more of the sun's heat is trapped and the earth's surface is warming up.

Atmosphere

What is a carbon footprint?

It is the impact you have on the planet. Each one of us has a carbon footprint, and so do all of the products we buy and use. When you watch TV, use the computer, or fly on an airplane, you probably use fossil fuels, so you add carbon dioxide and other greenhouse gases to the atmosphere. You can measure how much you produce from different activities. Buying food, clothes, and other things produced far away means that more fossil fuels are being burned to transport them, putting more greenhouse gases into the air. So having a small carbon footprint is much *better* for the planet than having a big one!

Greenhouse gases include carbon dioxide, methane, nitrous oxide, ozone, and water vapor.

How can we reduce our carbon footprint?

Switch it off!

The best way is to use less energy. We can start at home by turning down thermostats, hanging clothes out to dry rather than tumble drying them, and switching off lights, televisions, and computers when not needed. Transportation is another big carbon producer. So walking, cycling, or using public transportation really helps.

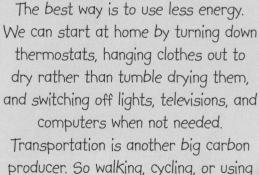

The carbon footprint of a cheeseburger

Find out how much carbon is emitted not only by cooking an average burger, but also by producing all the parts!

The pickles:
1/3 oz (9 g) of carbon to grow the cucumbers, cook the pickle mix, and transport and store

The onions:
1/2 oz (14 g) of carbon to grow, transport, and store

The cheese:
1 oz (40 g) of carbon to feed and milk the cows and make, transport, and store

The bun:
8 oz (226 g) of carbon to grow and transport the wheat, mill the flour, and bake and store

The lettuce:
1/3 oz (9 g) of carbon to grow, transport, and store

The beef:
4 lbs, 2 oz (1.86 kg) of carbon to grow the cattle feed, heat the cowsheds, slaughter the animals, and cut up, transport, grind, freeze, store, and cook

Countries around the world are trying to reduce greenhouse gas emissions and to find more sustainable ways of gathering energy and producing food.

How do plants live?

Plants live by producing food from the sun's energy. They make sugar from very simple ingredients: a bit of sunlight, water from the soil, and carbon dioxide from the air. Meanwhile, they release oxygen. This amazing process is called photosynthesis. Plants play a very important role on the planet. Without them, there would be no oxygen to breathe and no food for other living things. Animals (including us) eat plants, capturing the energy that originally came from the sun. Awesome, isn't it?

Carbon dioxide

Sunlight

Oxygen

Sunlight

Water

Sugar

Chloroplast
(contains chlorophyll, a chemical that absorbs sunlight)

Carbon dioxide

Oxygen

Plants produce food inside their leaves in tiny areas called chloroplasts. These chloroplasts trap energy from the sun, which reacts with carbon dioxide and water to make oxygen and sugar. This food travels out of the leaf to the rest of the plant.

Plants absorb carbon dioxide from the air and release oxygen.

Tree houses

Trees offer food and shelter to many insects, birds, and other animals. An old oak tree can be home to 350 different kinds of insects!

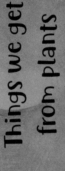

Things we get from plants

Can you imagine a world without chocolate, T-shirts, sugar, strawberries, guitars, and chewing gum? These wouldn't exist without plants. We eat their leaves, seeds, fruit, roots, and flowers. We use their fibers to make fabric and ropes. Some plants can be turned into medicines and perfumes. The remains of plants buried in the soil millions of years ago provide us with coal!

Why do leaves fall in the autumn?

Plants rest in the winter. They stop making food in the autumn when there is less sunlight and water. At this time, some plants drop their leaves, which conserves energy and water for the winter. Leaves change color because they stop producing chlorophyll (the chemical that absorbs sunlight and gives them their green color).

Every day, plants turn the sun's energy into millions of tons of sugar.

Timber!

We use trees to make all sorts of things: houses, furniture, toys, newspapers, and even this book. Wood is also burned as a fuel.

So long, soil!

Tree roots help hold the soil together. When trees are chopped down, the soil is more likely to get blown away by the wind or washed away by the rain. This makes it harder for plants to grow.

Water and nutrients

Trees are like giant water pumps. Their roots soak up water and nutrients, which they need to grow, from the soil. These travel up to the leaves, where water vapor escapes into the air.

Forests in danger!

Tropical rainforests are the air-conditioners of the earth. They soak up carbon dioxide from the air and release oxygen and water vapor. And they are home to more than half of the world's plant and animal species. Every two seconds, we clear an area of forest about the size of a football field to make space for farming, cattle ranching, and mining.

More than 20% of the world's oxygen is produced by the Amazon rainforest alone.

The dark green area shows how much of the Amazon rainforest remains. The red line shows the forest's original size.

Rotten logs and dead leaves are feasts for fungi, bacteria, insects, and worms. These creatures slowly return the dead plants' nutrients to the soil, helping new plants to grow.

What is a food chain?

A food chain is a group of living things that depend on each other for food. All plants and animals, including us, could one day be food for something else. Plants capture their energy from the sun, whereas animals eat plants or other animals as a source of energy. Dead plants and animals are food for fungi and bacteria.

A simple food chain

Producer

A food chain starts with a producer, usually a green plant. Plants use energy from the sun to produce their own food.

is eaten by the . . .

Primary consumer

Primary consumers only eat plants. They are also called herbivores.

A consumer is a creature that eats something.

which produces nutrients for the . . .

Pyramid of energy

This shows how energy is passed on as one living thing eats another. Energy is lost at each step of the food chain because animals use it to grow, move, or stay warm.

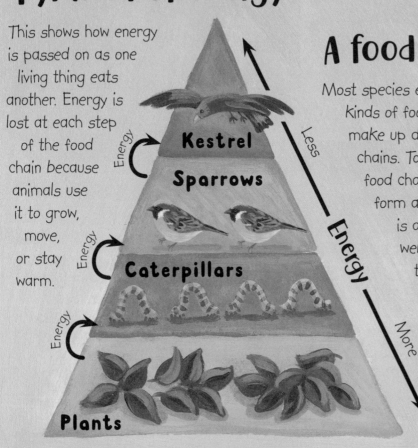

Kestrel

Sparrows

Caterpillars

Plants

Energy

Energy

Energy

Less Energy More

There are more caterpillars than sparrows because a sparrow must eat lots of caterpillars to get enough energy to survive.

A food web

Most species eat different kinds of food, so they make up different food chains. Together, all the food chains in a habitat form a food web. Here is a woodland food web. It could contain thousands of other different species— even you, maybe!

Cats
eat field mice and birds.

Field mice
feed on plants.

Foxes
eat field mice and snails.

Plants
are food for many animals as well as fungi.

Thrushes
eat slugs and snails as well as plants.

Slugs and snails
feed on plants and fungi.

What happens if you spray pesticides to get rid of the caterpillars that eat your plants? There'll be no food for the rest of the food chain!

Secondary consumer

eaten by the . . .

Secondary consumers eat the primary consumers. So, a sparrow might eat a caterpillar.

is eaten by the . . .

Tertiary consumer

Tertiary consumers eat secondary consumers. A bird of prey might eat another bird that has eaten a caterpillar. Birds of prey and other predators are called carnivores, which means meat-eaters.

Decomposer

is broken down by the . . .

When living things die, they become food for fungi and bacteria. These decomposers break down dead matter and return nutrients to the soil, which helps new plants to grow.

Wait a minute . . .
Don't some animals eat both plants and animals? Yes! Like bears and pigs, humans are omnivores, meaning we can eat everything.

Hawks
eat field mice and smaller birds, such as sparrows.

Sparrows
eat spiders and caterpillars.

Swallows
eat aphids.

Aphids
eat plants.

Spiders
eat caterpillars, aphids, and millipedes.

Caterpillars
feed on plants.

Fungi
feed on dead plants.

Millipedes
eat fungi.

What is bioaccumulation?

Polar bear

Poison!

Algae

Shrimp

Codfish

Seal

(Not as complicated as it sounds!) Factories and farms sometimes release poisons into the environment. Bioaccumulation is when these build up along the food chain. Because a codfish eats thousands of shrimp, the amount of poison in the fish will be larger than in a single shrimp. So a polar bear, at the top of the food chain, ends up with more poison in its body than any other creature along the chain.

Now that you know how the world works, discover . . .

How the **Weather** Works!

HOW THE

WEATHER

WORKS

christiane
Dorion

illustrated by
Beverley Young

How can balloons
measure the
weather?

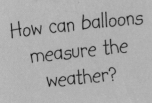

What's the link between cows
and our changing climate?